MW01224431

Phrasal Verbs

Peter Watcyn-Jones

Penguin Quick Guides Series Editors:
Andy Hopkins and Jocelyn Potter

Pearson Education Limited
Edinburgh Gate
Harlow
Essex CM20 2JE, England
and Associated Companies throughout the world

ISBN 0 582 46892 2

First published 2001
Second impression 2003
Text copyright © Peter Watcyn-Jones 2001

The moral right of the author has been asserted.

Produced for the publisher by Bluestone Press, Charlbury, UK
Designed and typeset by White Horse Graphics, Charlbury, UK
Illustrations by Jean de Lemos (Graham-Cameron Illustration)
Photographs on pages 33, 43, 53, 63, 73, 83, 95 and 107 by Patrick Ellis.
All others by Bluestone Press.
Printed and bound in China. NPCC/02

نام کتاب :	English Phrasal Verbs
ناشر :	انتشارات راهیان
نوبت چاپ :	اول
تیراژ :	۵۰۰۰ جلد
لیتوگرافی :	ثانیه
چاپ :	کیمیا
مرکز پخش :	انتشارات جنگل

Rahian Publications

021 - 6921166 - 6926639
0311- 2212047 - 6695337
0351- 6231378

Contents

8 **Health and fitness** 83

black out • break out • bring out • call up • change into
come down with • come out in • cut down • cut out
do without • get over • keep down • look up
make out • pack in • pick up • pull through • put off
put on • take out • throw up • turn up • work out

9 **Romance** 95

ask out • be cut up • break down • break up
burn down • carry on • come round • fall for
finish with • get along with • go down with • go off with
go out with • go through with • grow apart • let on
move in • pass out • put in • see through • stick by
walk out

10 **Bits and pieces** 107

Meeting people   bump into • call in • call round • drop by
drop in
Giving orders   get out • hang on • hurry up • look out
shut up • sit up
Daily life   get up • lie in • set off • turn off • wake up
School words   add up • bring out • get through
mess about
Weather words   brighten up • clear up • die down
start off

Getting
Started

What is a phrasal verb?

A phrasal verb is a main verb plus one or two particles.

Verb	Particle(s)
Go	away
Put	up with

Sometimes the meaning of the phrasal verb is clear because it is very similar to the main verb.

For example, the meaning of the words **stand** and **up** in the sentence opposite is easy to understand.

He **stood up** when she entered the room.

9

But often it is almost impossible to guess the meaning of a phrasal verb because it is very different from the meaning of the main verb.

Here, even if you understand **stand** and **up**, it doesn't help you very much.

*James **stood** me **up** last week.*
(= He failed to meet me after he had arranged to.)

Even if you learn the special meaning of a particular phrasal verb you can still have problems because sometimes a phrasal verb can have more than one meaning. Look at these.

*The plane **took off** (= left the ground) an hour late.*
*It's hot in here. Can I **take off** (= remove) my jacket?*
*James is good at **taking off** (= imitating) our teacher.*

So you really have to learn each phrasal verb as you see or hear it.

Why are phrasal verbs important?

To be really fluent in English you have to know phrasal verbs. They are an important part of the English language and particularly of the everyday language of spoken English.

What will I learn from this book?

This book concentrates on approximately 300 common and useful idiomatic phrasal verbs – i.e. phrasal verbs where the meanings are difficult to guess. You probably won't remember every phrasal verb in this book but I hope that you will manage to **pick up** (= learn) quite a few!

*I've **picked up** a lot of phrasal verbs today!*

Friends
and
family

1

Blood is thicker than water

get together

meet up

get on

fall out

count on

help out

I've got a very big family, but we **get together** less and less these days. In fact, we only **meet up** now when someone gets married.

Most of us **get on** with each other quite well. But my Uncle Dave is always **falling out** with people – especially his wife.

Families are strange. But at least you can **count on** them to **help** you **out** when you're in trouble. After all, 'Blood is thicker than water.'

*They don't seem to be **getting on** with each other very well these days.*

What is a good friend?

A good friend …

let down

- never **lets** you **down**.

stand by

stick up for

- always **stands by** you and **sticks up for** you when everyone else seems to be against you.

come out with

- always **comes out with** the truth – even when it hurts.

put up with

put up

- will **put up with** your bad moods … and will **put** you **up** when you miss the last bus home.

A good friend always **comes out with** the truth.

That hairstyle looks terrible!

A parent's promise

*Sometimes she thought she would **run out** of patience …*

I will try to ...

- **bring** you **up** to be happy.
- **look after** you when you are ill.

But I will ...

- **tell** you **off** when you behave badly.

I will try NOT to ...

- **take** my problems **out on** you.
- **run out** of patience with you – even when you're driving me crazy!

bring up

look after

tell off

take out on

run out

A teenager's threat!

*Dad's always **going on at** us about something.*

We will …

- always **answer** you **back**.
- never listen when you're **going on at** us.

We will not …

- **turn to** you when we need help.
- **look up to** you just because you're our parents.

But we will also try not to …

- **run away** when we've had enough.
- **end up** in trouble!

answer
back

go on at

turn to

look up to

run away

end up

Review 1

A Match the phrasal verbs with their meanings.

1 get together   a) quarrel
2 stand by   b) meet
3 fall out   c) admire, respect
4 look up to   d) support

B Fill in the missing phrasal verbs.

put up with   bring up   look after

1 Her mother died, so her father .... her .....
2 She treats him badly. How does he .... it?
3 She .... her parents when they were old.

C Are these true or false?

1 Most children enjoy being **told off**.
2 Friends should **stand by** each other.
3 Parents like their children to **run away**.
4 Kids should **answer** their parents **back**.

Holidays

2

Holiday plans

Things to do

1 Look at holiday brochures.

2 Pick the best holiday.

3 Make sure the passports haven't **run out**.

4 **Brush up** on the local language. Get hold of a good phrase book?

5 **Take out** enough money in traveller's cheques or foreign currency.

6 **Pick up** the tickets.

run out

brush up

take out

pick up

Tour guide

*Are you sure it will **take off**?*

We'll arrive at the airport at about 11 am and **check in** for the flight. The plane **takes off** at 1.30 pm and **touches down** in Naples about two hours later.

It'll be very hot there, so make sure you **put on** lots of suntan lotion.

Breakfast is served in your hotel, but for other meals you'll probably want to **eat out**. There are lots of restaurants to choose from in the town.

check in

take off

touch down

put on

eat out

A postcard home

*What do you mean, you've **left** the flag **behind**?*

Dear Mum,

What a disaster this holiday is **turning out** to be! I **left** my bag **behind** in the flat with my camera and most of my clothes. The plane was **held up** for three hours, so we didn't get to our hotel until 3 am! I haven't swum or sunbathed at all as it's rained non-stop every day so far. I'm **dying for** fish and chips as the food here is terrible! Will be really glad to **get back**!

Your loving son,

Dave

xxx

turn out

leave behind

hold up

die for

get back

Holiday advertisement

look forward to

get away from

go away

pop in

stop over

Looking forward to a holiday in the sun? Feel like **getting away from** it all? Can you **go away** in January or February? Then look no further.

Just **pop in** today to book your 'holiday of a lifetime' in Java – at a fabulous beach resort on the Indian Ocean. Holiday includes **stopping over** in Singapore for three days.

JAVA TRAVEL
18 High Street, Manchester

*They wanted to **get away from** it all!*

Review 2

A Match the phrasal verbs with their meanings.

1 take off   a) delay
2 get away from   b) leave the ground (plane)
3 hold up   c) escape

B Fill in the missing phrasal verbs.

look forward to   pop in   put on

1 Could you .... and see your mother on the way home?
2 We're really .... the summer holidays.
3 It's cold, so .... a warm jumper.

C Rewrite using these phrasal verbs.

pick up   die for   touch down   eat out

1 I *would really love* a cup of tea!
2 Don't forget to go and *fetch* the tickets.
3 We often *have meals at restaurants*.
4 Their plane *landed* at 2.30.

World
of
work

3

To work....

*I don't think he's really **cut out** for the part!*

RETURN OF SUPERHERO DIRECTOR

I don't think I'm really **cut out for** work. It seems to **take up** far too much of my free time. In fact, I **worked out** the other day that by the time I'm 65, I'll have spent nearly six million hours of my life working!

And I get so **snowed under** sometimes that I just refuse to **take on** any more work. I'd love to **give up** working. The only problem is – what would I have to complain about then?

be cut out for

take up

work out

be snowed under

take on

give up

ALFREDO THE LION TAMER

*The circus had to **cut back** on some things.*

Every day a factory somewhere **closes down** and every day someone gets **laid off** as companies are forced to **cut back** and rationalise.

And every day someone **thinks up** yet another way in which computers or robots can replace people.

In the future, being unemployed from time to time is something most people will have to **go through**, as the days of 'a job for life' (or even for a half of one's life) are long past.

close down

lay off

cut back

think up

go through

Newspaper headlines

*So you think your trouble started when your car mechanic business **went under**?*

GOVERNMENT TO **BRING IN** 6–HOUR WORKING DAY

NOKIA TO **TAKE OVER** MOTOROLA?

Union leaders **turn down** latest pay offer

One out of five new companies **go under** in their first year

NEW PLANS TO **DEAL WITH** UNEMPLOYMENT

bring in

take over

turn down

go under

deal with

Job advert

LOOKING FOR
A CHALLENGE?

Want an opportunity to
build up a new Internet
company from scratch?
If you feel you can **fit in**
with a young and dynamic
team of web designers
then visit our website to
find out more.
(You can even **fill in** our
online application form.)

www.IT_is_fun.com

look for

build up

fit in

find out

fill in

Review 3

A Match 1–3 with a–c.

1 I'm snowed under   a) this form.
2 Please fill in   b) this complaint.
3 Please deal with   c) with work.

B Fill in the missing phrasal verbs.

check in   cut out for   give up

1 Some people are not really .... marriage.
2 When do we ....?
3 It's really hard to .... eating meat.

C Are these true or false?

1 Big companies sometimes **take over** smaller ones.
2 Most people would be happy if they were **laid off**.
3 Successful factories don't usually **close down**.
4 Bosses prefer workers who don't **fit in**.

Leisure

4

A new hobby

*This game certainly helps to **let out** your frustrations!*

I've decided to **take up** golf. I never thought I would. To me golf had always been a sport for the rich and privileged. But as more and more of my friends started playing I **gave in** and decided to join them.

I played my first round a month ago. Now I'm hooked! I've really **taken to** it. It's a combination of a good walk plus the chance to **let out** your frustrations by hitting a ball rather than a person.

take up

give in

take to

let out

Soccer report

*What do you mean 'Why am I **sending** you off?'*

UNITED MARCH ON

Arsenal missed the chance of going to the top of the Premier League last night when they lost 4–1 to Manchester United. Despite **going ahead** 1–0 shortly after they **kicked off**, Arsenal never really looked like winning. United equalised two minutes before half time.

Midway through the second half two Arsenal players were **sent off**. Within minutes, United scored two goals. They **kept up** the pressure and **went on** to win 4–1.

go ahead

kick off

send off

keep up

go on

Newspaper headlines

It'll never catch on!

NEW STYLE OF TENNIS
RACKET SLOW TO **CATCH ON**

GRAND PRIX **CALLED OFF** AFTER
ACCIDENT DURING FIRST LAP

Plans for a European Super
League have **fallen through**

Injury forces England's captain to
pull out of vital World Cup match

MARATHON WINNER **OWNS UP**
TO TAKING DRUGS

catch on

call off

fall
through

pull out

own up

Sporting failures

By the time he finished the race, the stadium was **locked up**!

Some true stories …

Wallace Williams *(Virgin Islands)* ran so slowly in the 1979 Pan-American Games marathon, that by the time he got back to the stadium it was **locked up** and everyone had gone home.

Roberto Alvarez *(Mexico)* was so far behind in the 50-kilometres cross-country skiing race at the 1988 Winter Olympics, that worried officials **sent out** a search party to look for him.

Waving at the crowds after **coming in** fourth in the 500cc US Motor Cycle Grand Prix, Australian Kevin Magee **fell off** his bike and broke a leg.

lock up

send out

come in

fall off

Review 4

A Match the phrasal verbs with their meanings.

1 call off   a) confess
2 kick off   b) cancel
3 own up   c) like doing, enjoy
4 take to   d) start (e.g. a football match)

B Fill in the missing phrasal verbs.

take up   go on   send off

1 United .... to win 2–1.
2 I think you should .... some form of sport.
3 The referee .... the player .....

C Answer the following questions.

1 Can a horse **come in** last in a race?
2 Can plans **fall off**?
3 Can a runner **pull out** of a race?
4 Can a referee **send** a player **out**?

Cars
and
computers

5

Driving hints

drive off

pull out

slow down

cut in

pull up

Do …

- check your mirror before you **drive off** or **pull out** into traffic.

- **slow down** when driving in fog or when the roads are wet or icy.

Don't …

- **cut in** after overtaking other cars.

- **pull up** suddenly (e.g. at traffic lights, junctions or pedestrian crossings).

Don't **pull up** suddenly.

Car accident claims

When he tried to **pull away** he knew something was wrong.

Computers have minds of their own and always seem to **play up** or 'crash' at the worst possible moment. Most users find it impossible to work out exactly what has gone wrong, so it is very important that you regularly **back up** all your important files.

It is equally important that you **shut down** the computer correctly before you **switch off**. And whatever you do, don't forget to **log off** after using the Internet – otherwise your phone bill could be sky high.

play up

back up

shut down

switch off

log off

A computer genius?

He decided to **drop out** of school.

He **dropped out** of Harvard to **set up** a company with his friend Paul Allen. One of the first products they **brought out** was a version of BASIC for the Altair 8800 computer.

Then, in 1980, IBM asked them to **come up with** an operating system for their new personal computer. It was a huge success, and the company – Microsoft – went on to dominate the PC industry and make Bill Gates one of the richest and most powerful men in the world.

drop out

set up

bring out

come up with

Review 5

A Find a suitable ending for each phrasal verb.

1 back up   a) the light
2 bring out   b) important files
3 switch off   c) of college
4 drop out   d) a new magazine

B Fill in the missing phrasal verbs.

set up   cut in   play up

1 The driver …. sharply after overtaking the lorry.
2 My computer is …. .
3 Do you know who …. the company?

C Rewrite using phrasal verbs.

pull up   come up with   shut down

1 No one managed to *think up* any new ideas.
2 Do you think the factory will *close*?
3 The taxi *came to a stop* outside the station.

Money
and
shopping

6

Spending money

My kids are hoping to **come into** a fortune when I die.

I don't know many people who think they have enough money to **live on**. They **get by**, but very few seem able to **put aside** anything for the future. Again, thanks to credit cards, it is now very easy to **run up** huge debts which are very hard to repay. That's perhaps why so many people dream of **coming into** a fortune – usually by winning the National Lottery or the football pools.

live on

get by

put aside

run up

come into

Saving money

To **save up** for something (e.g. a new car) usually means having to cut back on things. You should try to:

save up

go without

splash out

stick to

- **go without** anything you don't absolutely need (CDs, new clothes, etc.)

- stop **splashing out** on expensive restaurant meals, visits to the cinema, pub, etc.

- decide on a fixed sum (e.g. £50) to save each month – and **stick to** it!

*I thought I'd **splash out** on a meal today.*

Easy money

*He **shut up** the bank and **moved on**.*

A true story …

Joseph Well, an American living in the early part of the 20th century, was a con man who **took in** so many people that he made over $6 million!

His favourite 'con' was to **open up** a new bank in a town, employ billiard room customers as cashiers and **fill up** cash bags with lead disks.

He would then convince businessmen that he had set up a genuine bank and wait for them to **pay in** large sums of money before **shutting up** and **moving on** to the next town!

take in

open up

fill up

pay in

shut up

move on

Shopping blues!

I'm just waiting for the prices to **come down** a bit more!

I hate shopping – especially for clothes. Just the thought of going into a clothes shop to **try on** something new is enough to **put** me **off**.

And to get the best bargains you really have to **shop around** or buy in the sales when prices really **come down**.

And even if you find something (e.g. a jacket), it's so hard to find a shirt to **go with** it. Or else the one you really wanted is **sold out**!

try on

put off

shop around

come down

go with

sell out

Review 6

A Match the phrasal verbs with their meanings.

1 come down   a) deposit (money)
2 pay in   b) save (money)
3 put aside   c) manage financially
4 get by   d) be reduced (e.g. prices)

B Fill in the missing phrasal verbs.

go with   splash out   take in

1 He was lying but I believed everything he said.
He really .... me .....
2 Do you think these shoes .... my skirt?
3 They really .... on their daughter's wedding.

C Are these true or false?

1 People don't usually like **coming into** money.
2 Some people are **put off** by the smell of garlic.
3 You can easily **run up** a big debt with a credit card.

Crime
and
punishment

7

Rising crime

*The defendant **got off** lightly.*

Crime and violence seem to be increasing. The newspapers are full of stories of people being **beaten up** or houses being **broken into**.

Most people would like the police and judges to **tighten up** on crime. Too many criminals seem to **get off** lightly – often they're just given a warning.

Even murderers are no longer **put away** for life but are often **let out** after 10 to 15 years.

beat up

break into

tighten up

get off

put away

let out

It's the law!

*You are not allowed to **get on** a plane within four hours of eating garlic!*

Strange US laws

- Anyone **setting off** a nuclear explosion within the city limits of Chico in California can be fined $500.

- Citizens in Wakefield, Rhode Island, are not allowed to **get on** a plane within four hours of eating garlic.

- Women who go to the hairdresser in Florida can be fined if they **drop off** under the hairdryer, while women in Minnesota can face up to 30 days in jail for **taking off** Santa Claus!

- Finally, in Newport, Rhode Island, it is illegal to smoke a pipe once the sun has **gone down**.

set off

get on

drop off

take off

go down

Crime doesn't pay ....

*The brick bounced back and **knocked** him out!*

Some true stories …

The police **picked up** Jack Kelim as he tried to **get away** on a bicycle after **holding up** a bank in Boulder, Colorado. Mr Kelim is 82 years old.

A thief tried to steal a necklace from a jeweller's shop in Detroit by throwing a brick at the window. Unfortunately for him, it was made of unbreakable glass, so the brick bounced back, hit him on the head and **knocked** him **out**. When he **came to**, he was under arrest in the local jail.

pick up

get away

hold up

knock out

come to

.... or does it?

*As he **picked up** the baby, he realised he'd been **set up**!*

Another true story ...

A woman with a pram walked into a jeweller's shop. Inside was a baby that **kept on** crying. But the jeweller didn't mind as the woman had **picked out** a very expensive ring for her husband who was sitting in their car parked round the corner. The jeweller agreed to look after the baby while she showed it to him.

keep on

pick out

pick up

set up

After a while he **picked up** the baby to stop it crying. What he found was a life-size doll and a tape recorder! The woman had **set** him **up**!

The woman got away with the crime. The police still haven't found her – or the £12,000 ring she stole!

Review 7

A Match the phrasal verbs with their meanings.

1	hold up	a)	fall asleep
2	take off	b)	continue
3	keep on	c)	rob (e.g. a bank)
4	drop off	d)	imitate

B Fill in the missing phrasal verbs.

get away   come to   break into

1 When she ...., she was in hospital.
2 Two teenagers .... the video shop.
3 The robbers .... in a blue Volvo.

C Answer Yes or No to the following questions.

1 Can you **get on** both a bus and a train?
2 Can you **let out** a car from a garage?
3 Can you **set off** an explosion by accident?
4 Can criminals be **put away** with just a warning?

Health
and
fitness

8

Keeping fit

My wife thought I should start **working out**!

I stopped playing football a few years ago when we had our first child – I just didn't seem to have the time. The trouble is, I've **put on** at least 5 kilos since then.

My wife thinks I should start **working out** and go on a diet. But that means **cutting out** sweets and chocolates. And it might mean **doing without** my daily glass of wine too!

Or perhaps I should stop worrying about **keeping** my weight **down**, and just be happy and fat!

put on

work out

cut out

do without

keep down

How to lose weight

I've managed to **cut down** on sweets.

- Make a list of the foods you want to stop eating.
- Choose a date to **pack in** the things on your list.
- Try to **cut down** before your target date, then stopping altogether will be easier.
- Replace sweets and fatty foods with fruit and fresh vegetables.
- **Call up** a friend and try to lose weight together.
- Come on, don't **put** it **off** any longer. Start today!

pack in

cut down

call up

put off

Newspaper headlines

*Don't worry, Mr Brown. I'm sure you're going to **pull through**!*

TYPHOID **BREAKS OUT** AFTER EARTHQUAKE IN ASIA

CHILD **PICKS UP** POLIO IN SWIMMING BATHS

Ambulance takes over an hour to **turn up** after emergency call

SOAP STAR MAY NOT **PULL THROUGH** AFTER OPERATION

Hundreds could **come down with** flu in the next few weeks

break out

pick up

turn up

pull through

come down with

Poor health

*I'm sorry, I don't remember anything. I must have **blacked out**!*

As we get older, we seem to get colds and other illnesses much more easily than before. It also seems to take us longer to **get over** them too.

My 85-year-old aunt had a terrible time last year. First she **blacked out**, fell and broke her leg. Then she got a gum infection and had to have all her teeth **taken out**. After that she got food poisoning and kept **throwing up**.

The good news? She **came out in** spots the other day, but it wasn't measles after all, just a heat rash!

get over

black out

take out

throw up

come out in

Growing old

*A broad mind and a narrow waist **changes into** a narrow mind and a broad waist!*

You know you're getting old when:

- the thought of a 'night out on the town' **brings** you **out** in a cold sweat.

- a broad mind and a narrow waist **changes into** a narrow mind and a broad waist.

- you have to **look up** old friends' numbers in the telephone directory because you've forgotten them, and then you can't **make** them **out** without glasses.

bring out

change into

look up

make out

Review 8

A Find a suitable ending for each phrasal verb.

1 come out in   a) sugar in coffee
2 call up   b) spots, a rash
3 cut out   c) an illness
4 get over   d) a friend

B Fill in the missing phrasal verbs.

put off   look up   cut down

1 I eat too much. I must try to .....
2 If you don't understand the word, ... it ....
   in a dictionary.
3 The meeting has been .... until next week.

C Are these true or false?

1 Most women are happy when they **put on**
   weight.
2 Poor handwriting is hard to **make out**.
3 People who **work out** are usually fit.

94

Romance

9

First love

*He's **fallen** for her in a big way!*

I first started **going out with** Nina when I was 19. We were both students. I **fell for** her in a big way – it was 'love at first sight'!

After a few weeks I finally **asked her out**. She said 'Yes'. That was it! By the end of term I was ready to spend the rest of my life with her.

A week later she **finished with** me! I **was** really **cut up**. How could she do this to me?

Looking back, it wouldn't have worked. But I still think of Nina sometimes. Well, you never really forget your first love, do you?

go out with

fall for

ask out

finish with

be cut up

Problems

*Sometimes couples just **grow apart**.*

Dear Abby,

My partner has just **walked out** on me. She says we've **grown apart** and is really tired of me. I can't understand it. I thought we **got along with** each other well. Since I **moved in** I've always taken her with me to watch Manchester United and I don't mind her joining me and my mates at the pub. And I never told her she was a terrible cook even though she was. I'm so surprised!

Let-down Barry

Dear let-down Barry,

The only surprise for me is that she's put up with you for so long!

walk out

grow apart

get along with

move in

Women on men

*Every time she **broke up** with a man she kept the house.*

- 'After a few years of marriage a man can look right at a woman without seeing her and a woman can **see** right **through** a man without looking at him.' *Helen Rowland*

- 'I am a marvellous housekeeper. Every time I **break up** with a man, I keep his house.' *Zsa Zsa Gabor*

- 'A girl must marry for love, and **carry on** marrying until she finds it.' *Zsa Zsa Gabor*

- 'They say girls tend to marry men like their fathers. That's probably why so many mothers **break down** at weddings.'

see through

break up

carry on

break down

... and men on women

*Everyone needs someone to **stick** by them in their troubles.*

- 'A wife is someone who'll **stick by** you in all the troubles you wouldn't have had if you hadn't married her.'

- 'I've had bad luck with both my wives. The first one **went off with** another man and the second one didn't.' *Patrick Murray*

- 'I married Miss Right. But she never **let on** before we got married that her first name was Always.'

- 'Take my advice. If you have any last-minute doubts about getting married, don't **go through with** it. Wait until you're absolutely sure.'

stick by

go off with

let on

go through with

A wedding day to remember

They spent their honeymoon **putting in** *a central heating system.*

A true story …

At a wedding in England in 1973 the vicar suddenly **went down with** flu and a replacement had to be brought in at the last minute.

Then the bride **passed out** as the ring was put on her finger and she didn't **come round** for 20 minutes.

The ceremony finally ended and the happy couple left in a van which contained a cement mixer. Their honeymoon hotel had **burnt down**, so they had decided to stay at home and spend the time **putting in** a new central heating system instead.

go down with

pass out

come round

burn down

put in

Review 9

A Match the phrasal verbs with their meanings.

1 go down with
2 pass out
3 put in

a) become ill with (a disease)
b) install (e.g. central heating)
c) faint

B Fill in the missing phrasal verbs.

cut up   burn down   go out with

1 Our hotel .....
2 How long has Jill been .... Andrew?
3 Helen was really .... when her cat died.

C Rewrite with phrasal verbs.

finish with   burn down   walk out (on)   stick by

1 Our house *was destroyed by fire* when we were on holiday.
2 Friends should *support* each other.
3 Tom has *ended his relationship with* Julie.
4 How could he *leave* his wife and two children?

Bits
and
pieces

10

Meeting people

*You can sometimes **bump into** a friend at the supermarket.*

There are so many different ways of meeting or visiting people.

- You can **bump into** them in the street or at the supermarket.

- You can tell them to **call round** and see you or to **drop by** one day when they're passing.

- Or you could always **call in** and see them, of course, as most people are happy when friends **drop in**.

bump into

call round

drop by

call in

drop in

Giving orders

shut up

get out

hurry up

hang on

sit up

look out

Hang on!
I'll get
help!

112

Sit up! You're in the army now!

Look out! Behind you!

Daily life

It's nice to lie in at the weekend.

Life's so boring, isn't it? You **wake up** every morning, **get up**, have breakfast and **set off** for work.

After a day at work, you come home, eat, watch TV and finally go to bed at about 11 o'clock. You read for a while, then **turn off** the light and try to go to sleep.

It's no wonder people look forward to the weekend when, instead of getting up early, they can actually **lie in** for a change.

wake up

get up

set off

turn off

lie in

School words

*Some pupils prefer to **mess about** in class.*

When you leave school you should be able to read, write and **add up**. School should also help to **bring out** and develop any special talents or abilities you have.

Unfortunately, not everyone is interested in school. Some pupils prefer to **mess about** in class rather than work. These pupils often drop out of school early.

But if you're clever and work hard, you'll probably **get through** your exams so you can go on to university.

add up

bring out

mess about

get through

Weather words

*The wind suddenly **died** down.*

The day will **start off** wet in most areas, but it should **clear up** in the afternoon. In the early evening it will **brighten up** – especially in Wales and the west.

Towards late evening, there could be heavy rain and high winds in the north of Scotland, which might even lead to some local outbreaks of thunder and lightning. But the wind should **die down** later on.

Temperatures will be between 15 and 17 degrees centigrade and the outlook for the next few days is rain and sunny spells for most parts of the country.

start off

clear up

brighten up

die down

Review 10

A Match 1–4 with a–d.

1 We set off for   a) and see me.
2 She got through   b) early.
3 Call in   c) the airport.
4 I always wake up   d) the exam.

B Fill in the missing phrasal verbs.

turn off   add up   clear up

1 What do you get when you …. 34 and 56?
2 She asked him to …. the light.
3 Do you think the weather will …. soon?

C Answer these questions.

1 Can you **drop in** and see a friend?
2 Are children who **mess about** in class popular with teachers?
3 Do people often **lie in** at weekends?

Phrasal
Verbs
Grammar

Phrasal verbs grammar

- Phrasal verbs have an effect on the structure of a sentence.
- Sometimes they are followed by an object; sometimes they are not.
- Sometimes the object appears between the verb and the particle.
- These letters are used as abbreviations in this chapter:

  $\boxed{\text{V}}$ verb $\boxed{\text{P}}$ particle $\boxed{\text{Pr}}$ preposition $\boxed{\text{Obj}}$ object

The following pages introduce seven main types of structure associated with phrasal verbs.

Type 1
Verb + particle

$\boxed{\text{V}}$ $\boxed{\text{P}}$

Margaret told the children to **hurry up**.
(= move more quickly)

In verbs of this type the particle follows the
verb. There is no object.

Some Type 1 verbs		
back down	*come round*	*get together*
break away	*die out*	*meet up*
come about	*end up*	*run away*

Type 2
Verb + particle + object

$$\overset{\boxed{V}}{looking} \;\; \overset{\boxed{P}}{after} \;\; \overset{\boxed{Obj}}{}$$

My parents are **looking after** my son.
(= taking care of him)

In this type, the particle is followed by an object – usually a pronoun or a noun phrase.

Some Type 2 verbs		
break into	*die for*	*pick on*
bring out	*fall for*	*stand by*
count on	*make for*	*take after*

Type 3
Verb + object + particle

$$\text{The song } \underset{V}{\textbf{took}} \underset{Obj}{\textit{John}} \underset{P}{\textbf{back}} \text{ to his childhood.}$$

(= reminded him of it)

In Type 3 phrasal verbs, the object usually comes between the verb and the particle in active sentences.

Some Type 3 verbs		
answer back	*hear out*	*let down*
call back	*help out*	*shut up*
count in	*keep down*	*stand up*

Type 4
Verb (+ object) + particle (+ object)

$$\underset{\text{V}}{\text{She }\textbf{turned}}\ \underset{\text{P}}{\textbf{on}}\ \underset{\text{Obj}}{\text{the lamp.}}$$

*She **turned on** the lamp.*

*She **turned** the lamp **on**.*

This is the most common type of phrasal verb.
The object can come before or after the particle.

> **Note** If the object is a personal pronoun (*him, me*, etc.)
> it MUST come before the particle. *She **knocked**
> **it over**. He **pulled** them **out**.*

Some Type 4 verbs		
add up	*knock out*	*switch off*
bring up	*put up*	*turn down*
give up	*show off*	*work out*

Type 5
Verb + object + particle + object

V Obj P   Obj

I'll **keep** you **to** your promise.

(= make sure that you keep it)

In this type, there is an object before and after the particle. Phrasal verbs of this type are not very common.

Some Type 5 verbs

hold against	*read into*
let into	*talk into*

Type 6
Verb + particle + preposition + object

$\boxed{V}$ $\boxed{P}$ $\boxed{Pr}$ $\qquad$ $\boxed{Obj}$

*Are you **going in for** the London Marathon?*
(= entering the race)

Phrasal verbs of this type are often called
'three-part' phrasal verbs because they have a
particle (always an adverb) AND a preposition.
Type 6 phrasal verbs are also followed by an
object.

Some Type 6 verbs

come down with	*go on at*	*put up with*
come out in	*go out with*	*stick up for*
get away from	*look up to*	

Type 7

Verb + object + particle
+ preposition + object

| V | Obj | P | Pr | Obj |

*Alan said his friend had **put** him **up to** it.*
(= encouraged him to do it)

These are also 'three-part' phrasal verbs but
unlike Type 6 verbs, an object also comes
between the verb and the particle. Type 7
phrasal verbs are not common.

Some Type 7 verbs		
do out of	*put down to*	*take out on*
let in for	*take up on*	*talk out of*

Using the Phrasal Verbs Index

Starting on the next page you will find the
Phrasal Verbs Index. Each verb in the Index is
followed by a number (1–7). This number tells
you which type of phrasal verb it is in terms of
grammar.

So, in the example below, **look after** is a
Type 2 phrasal verb.

> **look after** ② /lʊk ɑːftə/
> *She looks after her elderly mother.*

You can read about the grammar of **look after**
on page 124 under Type 2 phrasal verbs.

Phrasal
Verbs
Index

Your language

add up ☐ /æd ʌp/
Can you add up 37 and 94? _____

answer back ☐ /ɑːnsə bæk/
She answered the teacher back. _____

ask out ☐ /ɑːsk aʊt/
When he asked her out, she said 'Yes'. _____

back up ☐ /bæk ʌp/
Don't forget to back up important files. _____

be cut out for ☐ /biː cʌt aʊt fɔː/
I'm not really cut out for dancing. _____

be cut up ☐ /biː kʌt ʌp/
He was really cut up when his dog died. _____

be snowed under ☐ /biː snəʊd ʌndə/
I'm really snowed under with work. _____

beat up ☐ /biːt ʌp/
The two boys beat up the old man. _____

black out ☐ /blæk aʊt/
She suddenly blacked out. _____

Your language

break down ① /breɪk daʊn/
She broke down when her father died. _____

break into ② /breɪk ɪntuː/
The thieves broke into the flat. _____

break out ① /breɪk aʊt/
Chips make me break out in spots. _____

break up ① /breɪk ʌp/
He cried when Ann broke up with him. _____

brighten up ① /braɪtən ʌp/
It should brighten up in the evening. _____

bring in ④ /brɪŋ ɪn/
They're bringing in a new tax law. _____

bring out ④ /brɪŋ aʊt/
Sony have brought out a new camera. _____

bring out ④ /brɪŋ aʊt/
Nuts bring him out in spots. _____

bring out ④ /brɪŋ aʊt/
Diana brings out the best in James. _____

Your language

bring up ④ /brɪŋ ʌp/
She brought up four children. _____

brush up ② /brʌʃ ʌp/
I must brush up my French. _____

build up ④ /bɪld ʌp/
He built up the company himself. _____

bump into ② /bʌmp ɪntuː/
Sally bumped into him at the library. _____

burn down ④ /bɜːn daʊn/
Their house burnt down. _____

call in ① /kɔːl ɪn/
Call in and see me some time. _____

call off ④ /kɔːl ɒf/
The concert was called off. _____

call round ① /kɔːl raʊnd/
Call round and see me next week. _____

call up ③ /kɔːl ʌp/
John called me up on my birthday. _____

Your language

carry on ① /ˈkæri ɒn/
We carried on working until 3 am. _____

catch on ① /ˈkætʃ ɒn/
Will Internet phones catch on? _____

change into ② /tʃeɪndʒ ɪntuː/
The frog changed into a prince. _____

check in ① /tʃek ɪn/
What time do we have to check in? _____

clear up ① /klɪr ʌp/
The weather should clear up soon. _____

close down ④ /kləʊz daʊn/
They closed down the factory. _____

come down ① /kʌm daʊn/
House prices have come down. _____

come down with ⑥ /kʌm daʊn wɪð/
John's come down with flu. _____

come in ① /kʌm ɪn/
The favourite came in third in the race. _____

Your language

come into ② /kʌm ɪntə/
She came into money when he died. _____

come out in ⑥ /kʌm aʊt ɪn/
He came out in spots. _____

come out with ⑥ /kʌm aʊt wɪð/
He came out with a pack of lies. _____

come round ① /kʌm raʊnd/
He's unconscious. No! He's come round. _____

come to ① /kʌm tuː/
When she came to, she was in hospital. _____

come up with ⑥ /kʌm ʌp wɪð/
Microsoft came up with a new browser. _____

count on ② /kaʊnt ɒn/
You can always count on me. _____

cut back ① /kʌt bæk/
We need to cut back more. _____

cut down ① /kʌt daʊn/
I eat too much. I'll try and cut down. _____

Your language

cut in ① /kʌt ɪn/
The driver cut in after overtaking.　　＿＿＿＿＿

cut out ④ /kʌt aʊt/
She advised him to cut out sugar.　　＿＿＿＿＿

deal with ② /diːl wɪð/
She asked me to deal with the problem.　　＿＿＿＿＿

die down ① /daɪ daʊn/
Things should die down soon.　　＿＿＿＿＿

die for ② /daɪ fɔː/
He was dying for a cold drink.　　＿＿＿＿＿

do without ② /duː wɪðaʊt/
I'd find it hard to do without television.　　＿＿＿＿＿

drive off ① /draɪv ɒf/
The thieves drove off in a hurry.　　＿＿＿＿＿

drop by ① /drɒp baɪ/
They told us to drop by at any time.　　＿＿＿＿＿

drop in ① /drɒp ɪn/
People were always dropping in.　　＿＿＿＿＿

Your language

drop off ① /drɒp ɒf/
She was so tired she dropped off.

_____

drop out ① /drɒp aʊt/
She dropped out of university.

_____

eat out ① /iːt aʊt/
We eat out every night.

_____

end up ① /end ʌp/
He ended up in trouble.

_____

fall for ② /fɔːl fə/
She fell for him in a big way!

_____

fall off ② /fɔːl ɒf/
He fell off his motorbike.

_____

fall out ① /fɔːl aʊt/
Tom has fallen out with Maggie.

_____

fall through ① /fɔːl θruː/
Their plans have fallen through.

_____

fill in ④ /fɪl ɪn/
Could you fill in this form, please?

_____

Your language

fill up ④ /fɪl ʌp/
He filled up the bucket with water.

_____

find out ④ /faɪnd aʊt/
She tried to find out the answer.

_____

finish with ② /fɪnɪʃ wɪð/
She finished with him.

_____

fit in ① /fɪt ɪn/
She didn't fit in with the others.

_____

get along with ⑥ /get əlɒŋ wɪð/
Sally gets along with most people.

_____

get away ① /get əweɪ/
Stop them! They're getting away!

_____

get away from ⑥ /get əweɪ frɒm/
He tried to get away from the dog.

_____

get back ① /get bæk/
We got back at midnight.

_____

get by ① /get baɪ/
The family struggled to get by.

_____

Your language

get off ☐ /get ɒf/
The thief got off with a fine.

    _____

get on ☐ /get ɒn/
They got on the bus at the station.

    _____

get on ☐ /get ɒn/
The kids all got on with each other.

    _____

get out ☐ /get aʊt/
Get out! You're not allowed in here.

    _____

get over ☐ /get əʊvə/
She hasn't got over her dog's death.

    _____

get through ☐ /get θruː/
She gets through exams easily.

    _____

get together ☐ /get təgeðə/
We often get together at weekends.

    _____

get up ☐ /get ʌp/
What time do you get up?

    _____

give in ☐ /gɪv ɪn/
The wrestler refused to give in.

    _____

Your language

give up ④ /gɪv ʌp/
It's hard to give up smoking.

_____

go ahead ① /gəʊ əhed/
Spain went ahead 2–1.

_____

go away ① /gəʊ əweɪ/
Shall we go away at Easter?

_____

go down ① /gəʊ daʊn/
It's cooler once the sun goes down.

_____

go down with ⑥ /gəʊ daʊn wɪð/
He went down with flu.

_____

go off with ⑥ /gəʊ ɒf wɪð/
Tom's wife went off with his best friend.

_____

go on ① /gəʊ ɒn/
She went on to star in several films.

_____

go on at ⑥ /gəʊ ɒn ət/
He was always going on at her.

_____

go out with ⑥ /gəʊ aʊt wɪð/
He's going out with Jan.

_____

Your language

go through ② /gəʊ θruː/
He has gone through a lot this year. _____

go through with ⑥ /gəʊ θruː wɪð/
I can't go through with the operation. _____

go under ① /gəʊ ʌndə/
Five out of ten companies go under. _____

go with ② /gəʊ wɪð/
She bought a blouse to go with her skirt. _____

go without ② /gəʊ wɪðaʊt/
Could you go without beer for a month? _____

grow apart ① /grəʊ əpɑːt/
Husbands and wives often grow apart. _____

hang on ① /hæŋ ɒn/
Hang on! I'll be with you in a minute. _____

help out ④ /help aʊt/
He helps me out if I'm in trouble. _____

hold up ② /həʊld ʌp/
The train was held up for two hours. _____

Your language

hold up ④ /həʊld ʌp/
Two men held up a bank this morning. _____

hurry up ① /hʌri ʌp/
Hurry up or we'll miss the bus! _____

keep down ③ /ki:p daʊn/
You must keep your weight down. _____

keep on ① /ki:p ɒn/
Let's keep on working until 9. _____

keep up ④ /ki:p ʌp/
Arsenal kept the pressure up and won. _____

kick off ① /kɪk ɒf/
They kicked off at 3.30. _____

knock down ③ /nɒk daʊn/
He was knocked down near the bank. _____

knock out ④ /nɒk aʊt/
He knocked him out. _____

lay off ④ /leɪ ɒf/
The company has laid off 100 workers. _____

Your language

leave behind ③ /liːv bɪhaɪnd/
She left her passport behind.
_____

let down ③ /let daʊn/
Never let your friends down.
_____

let on ① /let ɒn/
He didn't let on that he was a soldier.
_____

let out ④ /let aʊt/
Who let the dog out?
_____

let out ④ /let aʊt/
You must let out your anger.
_____

lie in ① /laɪ ɪn/
I often lie in on Sundays.
_____

live on ① /lɪv ɒn/
They didn't have enough to live on.
_____

lock up ④ /lɒk ʌp/
Don't forget to lock the garage up.
_____

log off ① /lɒg ɒf/
Remember to log off from the Internet.
_____

Your language

look after ☐ /lʊk ɑːftə/
He often looked after the baby.
_____

look for ☐ /lʊk fɔː/
Excuse me, I'm looking for a toilet.
_____

look forward to ☐ /lʊk fɔːwəd tə/
We're looking forward to Christmas.
_____

look out ☐ /lʊk aʊt/
Look out, there's a car coming!
_____

look up ☐ /lʊk ʌp/
Look it up in a dictionary.
_____

look up to ☐ /lʊk ʌp tə/
I always looked up to my father.
_____

make out ☐ /meɪk aʊt/
What does this say? I can't make it out.
_____

meet up ☐ /miːt ʌp/
We usually meet up at Christmas.
_____

mess about ☐ /mes əbaʊt/
She always messed about at school.
_____

Your language

move in ③ /muːv ɪn/
At 18 she moved in with her friend. _____

move on ① /muːv ɒn/
They moved on to the next town. _____

open up ② /əʊpən ʌp/
The couple opened up a bank account. _____

own up ① /əʊn ʌp/
He owned up that it was his fault. _____

pack in ② /pæk ɪn/
I find it hard to pack in sweets. _____

pass out ① /pɑːs aʊt/
The soldier passed out in the heat. _____

pay in ④ /peɪ ɪn/
She paid in some money at the bank. _____

pick out ④ /pɪk aʊt/
They asked her to pick the thief out. _____

pick up ④ /pɪk ʌp/
They picked up the tickets. _____

Your language

pick up ④ /pɪk ʌp/
The thief was picked up by the police. _____

pick up ④ /pɪk ʌp/
He picked up the book from the floor. _____

pick up ④ /pɪk ʌp/
I picked up a tropical disease. _____

pop in ① /pɒp ɪn/
He popped in to the bank after work. _____

play up ① /pleɪ ʌp/
The television is playing up again. _____

pull away ① /pʊl əweɪ/
She slowly pulled away from the kerb. _____

pull out ① /pʊl aʊt/
He pulled out onto the main road. _____

pull out ① /pʊl aʊt/
She pulled out of the race. _____

pull through ② /pʊl θruː/
Will he pull through the operation? _____

Your language

pull up ☐ /pʊl ʌp/
The bus pulled up unexpectedly.
_____

put aside/by ☐ /pʊt əsaɪd/baɪ
She put aside/by £50 each month.
_____

put away ☐ /pʊt əweɪ/
Murderers should be put away for life.
_____

put in ☐ /pʊt ɪn/
We've decided to put in double glazing.
_____

put off ☐ /pʊt ɒf/
The strong smell of garlic put me off.
_____

put off ☐ /pʊt ɒf/
She put off the meeting until Friday.
_____

put on ☐ /pʊt ɒn/
Remember to put on some sun cream.
_____

put on ☐ /pʊt ɒn/
She put on weight in the winter.
_____

put up ☐ /pʊt ʌp/
Don't go to a hotel. I'll put you up.
_____

Your language

put up with ⑥ /pʊt ʌp wɪð/
How does she put up with him? _____

run away ① /rʌn əweɪ/
He ran away because he was unhappy. _____

run into ② /rʌn ɪntuː/
She ran into a tree in the dark. _____

run out ① /rʌn aʊt/
Her passport had run out. _____

run over ④ /rʌn əʊvə/
The man accidentally ran over a cat. _____

run up ④ /rʌn ʌp/
My sister ran up a huge debt. _____

save up ① /seɪv ʌp/
I'm saving up for a new car. _____

see through ② /siː θruː/
He's a liar. I can see through him. _____

sell out ① /sel aʊt/
The tickets for the concert are sold out. _____

Your language

send in ④ /send ɪn/
She sent in her application form. _____

send off ③ /send ɒf/
He was sent off for fighting. _____

send out ④ /send aʊt/
They sent out thousands of brochures. _____

set off ④ /set ɒf/
The alarm was set off by accident. _____

set off ① /set ɒf/
They set off for France. _____

set up ④ /set ʌp/
The company was set up by two people. _____

set up ④ /set ʌp/
The con men had set him up! _____

shop around ① /ʃɒp əraʊnd/
Shop around to get the best bargains. _____

shut down ④ /ʃʌt daʊn/
...y are shutting down the factory. _____

Your language

shut up ④ /ʃʌt ʌp/
The cinema has been shut up for years. _____

shut up ① /ʃʌt ʌp/
Shut up! I'm trying to work. _____

sit up ① /sɪt ʌp/
Sit up properly when you're eating. _____

slow down ① /sləʊ daʊn/
Mary slowed down at the lights. _____

splash out ① /splæʃ aʊt/
He's very mean and never splashes out. _____

stand by ② /stænd baɪ/
He stood by her in times of trouble. _____

start off ① /stɑːt ɒf/
It will start off fine in most areas. _____

stick by ② /stɪk baɪ/
They stuck by each other. _____

stick to ② /stɪk tə/
When you make a decision, stick to it. _____

Your language

stick up for 6 /stɪk ʌp fə/
Only one person stuck up for him. _____

stop over 1 /stɒp əʊvə/
Did you stop over in Dubai? _____

switch off 4 /swɪtʃ ɒf/
Could you switch off the light, please? _____

take in 3 /teɪk ɪn/
Some people are easily taken in. _____

take off 1 /teɪk ɒf/
The plane took off on time. _____

take off 2 /teɪk ɒf/
James loved taking off his teachers. _____

take on 4 /teɪk ɒn/
Corus are taking on more workers. _____

take out 4 /teɪk aʊt/
She took out some money. _____

take out 4 /teɪk aʊt/
How many teeth did he take out? _____

Your language

take out on ⑦ /teɪk aʊt ɒn/
He took his anger out on her. _____

take over ④ /teɪk əʊvə/
They plan to take over the company. _____

take to ② /teɪk tə/
Her son really took to tennis. _____

take up ② /teɪk ʌp/
This job takes up too much time. _____

take up ② /teɪk ʌp/
Tom decided to take up jogging. _____

tell off ④ /tel ɒf/
His mother told him off for swearing. _____

think up ④ /θɪŋk ʌp/
Who thought up the idea? _____

throw up ① /θrəʊ ʌp/
He drank too much and threw up. _____

tighten up ② /taɪtən ʌp/
We need to tighten up security. _____

Your language

touch down ① /tʌtʃ daʊn/
The plane touched down safely. _____

try on ④ /traɪ ɒn/
Would you like to try it on for size? _____

turn down ④ /tɜːn daʊn/
She turned down the job in Canada. _____

turn off ④ /tɜːn ɒf/
Could you turn off the light, please? _____

turn out ① /tɜːn aʊt/
The weather turned out nice. _____

turn to ② /tɜːn tə/
He turned to her for help. _____

turn up ① /tɜːn ʌp/
What time did Jenny turn up? _____

wake up ① /weɪk ʌp/
I usually wake up at about 7.30. _____

walk out ① /wɔːk aʊt/
My wife walked out on me last week. _____

Your language

work out ④ /wɜːk aʊt/
Can you work out the answer?   _____

work out ① /wɜːk aʊt/
She usually works out twice a week.   _____

Answers

Review 1

A 1b 2d 3a 4c
B 1 brought (her) up 2 put up with 3 looked after
C 1 false 2 true 3 false 4 false

Review 2

A 1b 2c 3a
B 1 pop in 2 looking forward to 3 put on
C 1 I'm dying for a cup of tea.
   2 Don't forget to go and pick up the tickets.
   3 We often eat out.
   4 Their plane touched down at 2.30.

Review 3

A 1c 2a 3b
B 1 cut out for 2 check in 3 give up
C 1 true 2 false 3 true 4 false

Review 4

A 1b 2d 3a 4c
B 1 went on   2 take up   3 sent (the player) off
C 1 Yes, it can.
   2 No, they can't. (But they can fall through.)
   3 Yes, they can.
   4 No, he can't. (But he can send a player off.)

Review 5

A 1b 2d 3a 4c
B 1 cut in   2 playing up   3 set up
C 1 No one managed to come up with any new ideas.
   2 Do you think the factory will shut down?
   3 The taxi pulled up outside the station.

Review 6

A 1d 2a 3b 4c
B 1 took … in   2 go with   3 splashed out
C 1 false   2 true   3 true

Review 7

A 1c 2d 3b 4a

B 1 came to   2 broke into   3 got away

C 1 Yes, you can.
  2 No, you can't. (But you can let an animal out
    of a cage.)
  3 Yes, you can.
  4 No, they can't. (But they can be put away in
    prison for a long time.)

Review 8

A 1b 2d 3a 4c

B 1 cut down   2 look (it) up   3 put off

C 1 false   2 true   3 true

Review 9

A 1a 2c 3b

B 1 burnt down   2 going out with   3 cut up

C 1 Our house burnt down when we were on holiday.
  2 Friends should stick by each other.
  3 Tom has finished with Julie.
  4 How could he walk out on his wife and two
    children?

Review 10

A 1c 2d 3a 4b

B 1 add up 2 turn off 3 clear up

C 1 Yes, you can.
   2 No, they aren't.
   3 Yes, they do.

Other titles available in Penguin Quick Guides